CROSSING BORDERS

For Bennett
with warmest wishes

Peter
March 3, 2007

Also by Peter Dale Scott
  Available from New Directions:

Coming to Jakarta (1989)
Listening to the Candle (1992)

CROSSING BORDERS

Selected Shorter Poems

Peter Dale Scott

A NEW DIRECTIONS BOOK

Manufactured in the United States of America
New Directions Books are printed on acid-free paper
Published by arrangement with Véhicule Press, Montreal, Canada
First published as New Directions Paperbook 796 in 1994

Library of Congress Cataloging-in-Publication Data

Scott, Peter Dale.
    Crossing borders : selected shorter poems / Peter Dale Scott.
        p.   cm.
    ISBN 0-8112-1284-X
    I.   Title.
PR9199.3.S364C76   1994
811'.54—dc20   94-20526
                                                                                                  CIP

The following poems are reprinted.
    From *Modern Canadian Verse* (Toronto: Oxford University Press, 1967): "Argenteuil
County," "The Loon's Egg." From *Rumors of No Law* (Austin: Thorp Springs Press, 1981):
"Prepositions of Jet Travel," "My Son Rowing," "Dying In," "Talks at the Yenan Forum,"
"I Hate Modern Poetry," "Sora," "Almond Tree," "Eagle." Most of these poems, together
with "Watch," were also published in the chapbook *Prepositions of Jet Travel* (Berkeley:
Berkeley Poetry Review, 1981). From the chapbook *Heart's Field* (Berkeley: Aroca Press,
1986): "Free Climb," "Flight," "Olive Oatman," "Merced Canyon," "Carnass." From
the *Berkeley Poetry Review*: "Talks at the Yenan Forum," "Dying In," "Mischievousness,"
"Coppetts Wood Hospital," "Reflections on a Fifty-Eighth Birthday," "Ephemeris,"
"Max Scherr's Party," "Sora," and "Almond Tree." From *Brick*, "Flight." From *The Harvard
Review*: "Letter to Paul Alpers."
    The story of Olive Oatman, as presented in the diary of Susan Thompson Lewis
Parrish, as well as her photograph from the collection of the Arizona Historical Society,
will be found in Lillian Schlissel, *Women's Diaries of the Western Journey* (New York: Schocken
Books, 1982), 67-71. This book is said to have been one of four at the bedside of
President Reagan.

New Directions Books are published for James Laughlin
by New Directions Publishing Corporation,
80 Eighth Avenue, New York 10011

For Alan Williamson

CONTENTS

I
HEART'S FIELD

II
LAURENTIAN ECLOGUES

III
RUMORS OF NO LAW

IV
MOUNT TAM

V
SPACE SONNETS

VI
MIDDLE KINGDOM

VII
COAST TRAIL

HEART'S FIELD

OLIVE OATMAN

[From the diary of Susan Thompson Lewis Parrish, 1850]

When Mrs. Oatman was
seized with the pains of childbirth
no one noticed the approach

of 17 Apache braves
who murdered her her husband
and three youngest children

and like the heroes
of Homer's *Iliad*
carried away Olive and Mary Ann

The rest of us continued
on reaching California
we opened a hotel

at the age of fifteen
I soon married
an emigrant from New York

who had stopped for a night's rest
Many years later
They found the girl

in her bark dress
seated
on the river bank

At the approach
of the white men
she buried herself

in the sand

    ii

The Apaches had sold her
to a Mohave
for blankets

At every opportunity
she sought
to flee back to her Indian

husband and children
For four years
she lived with us

a grieving
unsatisfied woman
who somehow shook one's belief

in civilization
In time we erased
the tatoo marks from her face

but not the wild life from her heart
Perhaps we were wise
in sending her to Oregon

She must have forgotten
as the years went by
for in time she married

a Mr. Fairchild
a banker from Texas

iii

In her tight-waisted
Victorian gown
and black ringlets

she rests one ladylike
hand on the highback chair
embroidered with needlepoint

and stares out far
beyond the shoulder
of the unseen cameraman

The black crisscrossed
lines around her cuffs
and around her hem

imitate the style
of the black hatchmarks
between her chin and lips

which lasted a lifetime
made by piercing the skin
and pressing charcoal

into the wounds

MERCED CANYON

After these many false starts
    we are dispirited although
  this seems right a sphagnum meadow

smelling of wild onions
    under the vertical granite
  just like the ranger said

so we explore the flat
    crest of rock outside it
  strewn with duff and boulders

too random to have had
    any obvious intention
  until I call out *Here*

is the grinding-stone and at once
    we wonder how we could have missed it
  the symmetrical pestle standing

by itself in the skin-smooth hollow
    of the abraded rock
  it fits from so much practice

We take off our dark glasses
    and bit by bit the ground
  glints with the obsidian flakes

we had been looking for
    till they are everywhere and together
  reflect the empty heroic sky

I go back to the scooped-out pool
        in the frost-withered lupines
    where we first crossed the brook

and kneel where the bank is flattened
        the water just as musical
    the inverted cliffs

as clear as they ever were
        while behind me
    on the other side of the canyon

drifts the white smoke
        of the small forest fire
    they are letting burn

MOUNT VOGELSANG

We leave our packs in the stunted
    whitebark pine and prepare
  to go up the chute

which proves to be a cinch
    I forget my altitude sickness
  we know we are reaching the crest

from the first smell of woodsmoke
    out of Merced Canyon
  and now on the south side

it is nothing but a hike up
    until just below what must be
  the peak giddiness too few

ledges to stand on
    so I go first and cling
  to the final overhang

thank God it is solid
    I get one leg on top
  and then as if at last

I have got a handle
    on the edge of the planet
  I pry it and myself

towards each other
    an entire new landscape
  lurches up at me

will not settle down despite
      my effort to recognize
   the long smudge through Tioga Pass

and the glints of Tuolumne Meadows
      as the small open secret
   of our immediate past

invading to no clear purpose
      the ignorant mountains
   and the still smaller flash

of a falcon hovering
      down at eleven thousand feet
   till after five minutes

if only to get straight
      at last which is on top
   I stand up as carefully

as would a small child
      for the first time
   on the capstone

at the exact center
of the admiring world

FREE CLIMB

To Maylie

Climbing to 37,000 feet
above Yosemite
and the ABC Sportsflight

shows the first free climb
of the Lost Arrow Spire
directly beneath me

so steep above the window
of the Ahwahnee Restaurant
we had to twist our necks

up to the two roped mites
probably not these
just as the announcer

says *this morning* but
it cannot be *this* morning
his helicopter perspective

of the watery canyon
not as high as mine
the eggs and sausage arriving

above the thunderclouds
as the lead climber falls
the length of his belay

enough to bite his tongue
blood over his hand
and I as suddenly

am close to a cold sweat
once on Mont Saint Hilaire
above the white wood crosses

fully extended on a similar
rockface I had to drop
hoping to catch the ledge

saved by a chance handhold
for a sedate career And yet
my trip to the Archives

to finish this manuscript book
about Mengele and the US
in Latin America

years after the cold
breakfast in the drizzle
with the Canadian film-maker

outside the gates at Auschwitz
is in its way a first
crack at an unscaled pitch

no summit visible
learning to climb free
You must be half way

to Tassajara
our daughter sleeping
on the madrone hillside

above Suzuki Roshi's grave
as I add you to this margin
of my manuscript notebook

he reaches the flat top
and spreads his arms
laughing in my headset

from needless relief
in this country
we make our own risks

even beside this window
I am in my quiet way
engaged with power

my phone line tapped again
as during Vietnam
the stewardess laughing

as she pours me coffee
from the tapestry blue
mountains of Guatemala

and Sandoval's death squads
trained by ex-Nazis
where in my last chapter

we murder the Indians
whose embroidered serapes
are older than Columbus

high high above
a storm in the Wasatch
I remember the driving

rain and hail across
the top of the Pyrenees
where the map had promised shelter

but the hostel as we struggled
wearily towards it
had been totally bombed out

from what I learned by chance
searching Catalan journals
more than fifteen years later

for Romanesque art and verse
was a raid on the refugees
fleeing into France

in the last air attack
of the Spanish Civil War
in innocence mindful

only of life's weather
not the buried corpses
my idle left hand

switches the announcer
into leaping strings
hilaritas

the friendly schmaltz
composed here in Iowa
of Dvorak's imagined

New World

EPHEMERIS

To Ausonius (ca. 310-393 A.D.)

OWL COTTAGE

fish pier lights
      through the eucalyptus
   slow breath beside me

time to rise

RUNNING THE FIRE TRAIL

jagged ridge's
      yin frosts yang warmths
   each outside bend

another sunrise

BREAKFAST

ding! toast
      and the steam of oolong
   poured just so each morning

thirty years

COMPUTER TERMINAL

behind my face's ghost
      my memory
   whatever I most want

saved!

CLASS

once more in the amphitheater
        to teach how Odysseus
    pulled off the genitals   Odyssey 22.477

Nicaragua

TRAFFIC

at 5 m.p.h.
        Handel. She said *at first*
    I considered it time lost

and then   a kind of gift

EVENING ZA-ZEN

once thirsty seeking water
        now late   how not to spill
    this too full

bowl

CANDLELIGHT

moon over ground fog
        a eucalyptus nut
    startles the roof

and at last   owls

FLIGHT

For Frank Scott, d. January 31, 1985

I

From his hospital bed
his hair neatly parted by the nurse
and his kleenex folded into eighths

held taut between his hands
my father watches the television
movie they made of him

only twelve months ago
The reception is bad
but it does not matter

my father is not concerned
with the kindly images
the world and the movie camera

have registered There are
deeper voices inside himself
with rages he does not care for

or recalling the future
from the distant past

II

you should have seen Peter
when he was a little boy
he would fly right up to the wire fence

with mesh holes in it
no bigger than your fist
but his eyes were so good

he would fly right through the hole
without his wings touching
the wire on either side

and then vanish
When was this Frank?
Before either you or I

were born

III

| årit | kheperu | em | ment |

(Book of the Dead, lxxxvi)

Frank, I should read you what it says
about making the transformation
into a *ment*-bird

I am a ment-*bird*
I have travelled with an order
How shall I tell what I have seen?

I stretched out my two arms
I passed on to judgment
I am pure at the place of passage

May I come forth from the sektet *boat*
and may my heart be brought to me
from the mountain of the east

May I gather myself together
as the beautiful golden hawk
and may the sacred wheat

be given me for my eating

IV

I had come into the room
to say good-bye
You are propped into your chair

in exact alignment
with the landscape of glaciers
at the head of the bed

You do not wish to talk
you tell me you have
no time to waste

on mere recitations
and then with elaborate
ceremony and suspense

you kiss your knees

WATCH

For John Marshall, d. September 26, 1980

John as I planned my lecture on Aeneas
        carrying old Anchises on his neck
    I felt the new weight of your watch

hanging loosely from my wrist
        its hands told me
    with unnecessary precision

in five minutes
        it will be one your time
    cremation time

If I am to say something
        at this Homeric moment
    I must write quickly

which might be easier
        than when you were alive
    but is no substitute

for our postponed discussion
        about conspiracies
    and the Rockefeller Foundation

you served perhaps too well
        just as at the watch store
    they were surprised at what good care

you had taken of it
        so much order outlasted
    the good times at Bog Lake

where in the family cabin
        you served daughter and would-be son-in-law
    your own fresh-caught trout

the chickens you caponized yourself
        the mushrooms you grew from dung
    the steaks you arranged for from the Machias butcher

years later the cabin sold
        it was not the same somehow
    in the Villa Serbelloni

catering to tamed ex-Trotskyites
        NATO intellectuals
    eminent academics

and even for one brief
        humiliating weekend
    the President of the United States

When Dean Rusk did not
        as you had predicted
    clean up the Vietnam War

you began your two-volume
        history of the villa
    the raid of Theodoric the Goth

the columns of Pliny the Younger
       which in the end they failed to publish
    just as they stopped

your bottlings of the estate wines
       from the terraced vineyards
    leaving you the sybaritic

discussions of menus with Vincenzo
       and occasional tastings
    of watery 1889 Laffitte

Imprisoned in this monument
       of your partial success
    you waited for your retirement

for that evening you and Maylie sat outside
       on the deck above the maples
    to have a talk

and the only sound
       as the pale sun danced
    in your unsteady sherryglass

was the rustle
       among the scattered birdseed
    of the nervous grosbeaks

while the watch ticked inaudibly
       the hours and days away
    from those first *cénacles* at Harvard

where you practiced gastronomy
    with your deipnosophist
    poet room-mates

your Beowulf so interpaginated
>with your glosses from Professor Kittredge
>in Anglo-Saxon and Old Norse

I still teach from it
>*seolfa ne cuðe* he himself knew not
>*or Men ne cunnon*

secgan to soþe   selerædende
>*hæleð under heofenum   hwa þæm hlæste onfeng*
>men cannot

say the truth   hall-counselors
heroes under heaven   who received that cargo

CAMASS

Idaho: October 6, 1985

For Dick and Mary Anderson, Mary de Rachewiltz, Olga Rudge

"The drive was delightful and merry the scenery fine at one eminence we had a picture before us like Bierstadt's Rocky Mountains....The entrance to Camas Prairie is down a steep narrow gulch prettily surrounded with a stream beside the roadway, looking down the gully to the Prairie I could but think of the old patriarchs looking over into the Land of Canaan....We drove twenty miles on the Prairie stayed overnight at the Inn of Soldier where the lands belonging to various members of the family are situated it is all fine farm land rich and level and there are many settlers all about.... Homer and Mr. Foote have fenced forty acres each to protect the nuts planted." — Isabel Pound, May 1885

Too late to change *heart's field?*   Canto 111. p. 782
        Mary's plane at eleven
    Dick and I in the back-up car

coming down through hills of lava
        as Isabel did in 1885
    to visit the homesteads

the Inn of Soldier
        old carved door in the new siding
    old woman living on oxygen

a question of time
        tomorrow, the page proofs, in Milan
    no sleep last night the scholar

replaying the broadcasts
        in the static, the terrible
    fight with words

(*Noh Drama*
    pogrom)
    and Shoshone Indians coming

each spring, to gather camass
        till the last war
        the last lava flow

shifting the Wood River west
        out of its valley
        harrier's long low gliding

beaver dams in the stream
        before any of this
        watched for sagegrouse

saw mountain bluebirds
        and yellow aspens
        Dick: *the wagons*

must have come down in the streambed
        Isabel: *the old patriarchs*
        into the Land of Canaan

to die in the Sudtirol
        peace? or a painted prospect?
        salmon lost at the barriers

in a conflict of jurisdictions?
        or the snow geese protected
        to save the swans?

sì wú xié   think no depravities
think: heart's field   *Analects*, II.ii

31

GRIN

a glimpse of the skull

LETTER TO CZESLAW MILOSZ

October 27, 1982

Dear Czeslaw,
    Dreams once of the future
become the past. I am not likely
ever to take you to the unsecret
exposed hill in the nearby Briones
where someone saw two golden eagles mating,
or collect and then make for you a soup
of cress from the small brooks where they empty
into the Pacific. And yet
I have never been more in need of a friend, a man
not to agree with — agreement
only makes me the more anxious —
but whom I can watch survive, far from
birthplace and original heroic causes.
    I used to think of you as a giant
Jeffers-like lighthouse on its quirky secure crag:
a lighthouse not much use
for reading small print by or exploring
the local landscape, but a beacon
reaching far out to sea, and into time,
punctuating the usual darkness with
occasional unnatural light
perhaps too bright close up, but a godsend
to ships foundering, and those whose life
seems over-menaced in small unaccustomed
lifeboats. Sometimes the pleasant
company I am seldom without
seems, when I look up and see waves,
a threat to survival. Even my wife
after a quarter century, I begin to admit

has her own problems of another sex
to deal with, inscrutable. Thus alone
in the midst of friends, I need to know
what it is your strange eyes have seen
out there in the night.
        So I read your books. This is the way
it should be. Face to face
those years we translated Herbert
and so many others, word
by recalcitrant word, translation proved
a more intimate, because more demanding,
intercourse than mere natural speech
in a single language: the distance
between our tongues defined them
the more closely, a parallax
to peer beyond night's surface, give an edge
so sharp to our words that, handled by two,
they became dangerous; and, turned
on the sensitive flesh of your own poems,
could only draw blood.
            I have come to think
having watched others who also came close
it was that transgression
of your intimacy, which led
to my no longer seeing you — and not,
as I first thought, our hopeless disagreement
over the Vietnam War (although that hurt,
your pointed jibe at, not myself, but Chomsky,
on whose platform you had seen me sitting:
one of those intellectuals of no sense
who destroyedWeimar).
            I never expected
silence after that outburst. For me
divergence over how "to defend the west"
was a small matter, almost parochial.

I have always had trouble choosing sides.
That takes experience. I am tempted
even today, with fresh news of strikes
in Nowa Huta and Bydgoszcz, to wish compassion
for all those, including the oppressors,
who move from so little choice,
though I can see how much more severe
I am in judging America's repressions.

Your defection from the diplomatic
came after friends had gone to jail, or
elegantly accommodated lies, while foreign
troops lurked in the western forests.
To you, my philosophizing
must seem demented, when the issue
is not just brute stupidity but enslavement:
just as, in this book, you scorn the unhappy
youth who asked *how life in Sacramento
differed from a concentration camp.*

In your book there is fear
of *orgies of masochism*, revolutionary
students with walkie-talkies (as if the police
could not jam those scratchy plottings at their will)
or *nearly suicidal freedom
of expression.* But then you wrote
of that Catholic or Marxist in yourself
that wished to censor what you had written about,
de Sade, because words are important
(*Who has not dreamt of the Marquis de Sade's châteaux?*),
and the hellish aura of the ghettos burning
on the living-room t.v., so toxic
that our escape is *in brutish
contemplation like a cow.* Your true fear
was of your own ferocity; in this
you spoke to the censorious libertine
in each of us, even if

some of us would not censor but correct.
And of something else (Vietnam!) your sense was *tragic*:
you wanted neither side to win.

      Strange, just yesterday,
to find what you must have written
long before that final sunny noon
in Sproul Plaza we crossed by accident,
the first time in two years. The war
was going badly then, and you imputed
to me, with gruffness, some contrary opinion,
some joy I did not feel. I said *No,
my view of this was always tragic*, and you relented;
we talked for two hours on the terrace
over coffee, though I did not then dare
to tell you how much I missed
the long drinking nights of translation
at your house, overlooking the stars
and shiplights in the bay: Herbert, Wat,
Mandelstam, the peasants of Lithuania,
until you fell forward in your chair, and Janka,
at that exact moment, slipped from behind a door
to tell me to go home.

               Drunk myself
I would inch homeward on the winding
crest of Grizzly Peak, through fog as dense
as my confusion. Strange single branches then,
that hung out of the swirling wet white,
the silhouette of a fawn above my headlights,
or the ping on my Peugeot roof
of a eucalyptus nut, would strike on my senses
the marks of a signed universe. Always
what I saw, after talking to you,
was like, only more than, what the door frames
as you leave an art museum.
And for the first time, in my mid-career,

anything seemed possible.

     I did not tell you this
because we were face to face; and you
I believe are like what I have become,
perhaps what we all become:
someone you can only be close to
by keeping far enough away. If others
translate with you now, and are not rejected,
I would like to think they are too different
to be estranged, having lived
only in one country, being too much poets
to have, like us, wrestled the ideas
of Massis, Curtius, and Benjamin,
above all, too knowledgeable to wish,
any more than Horace would, to change the world.
You have *no ambition to save the world*,
and yet, thank god, you grumble
continuously about salvation:
umysł ludzki jest wspaniały, usta potężne,
i wezwanie tak wielkie, że musi otworzyć się Raj
the human mind is splendid, lips powerful,
and the summons so great, it must open Paradise.

     We are of course all alien out here,
where, as you wrote, your accent made you normal.
This strangeness I am used to
from my so-called native land, yet nonetheless
it gave me unasked-for roots, and roots
(above all roots one is in flight from)
are what distinguishes the emigré.
I was the rustic who sat at your feet,
having come, as you did, out of the black north
to visit the huddled cities of Europe,
or even the soft vineyards of the Pacific,
as a querulous appreciative stranger.
And I thought of you at the salons

of your odd Parisian cousin, so jolted
by what you were only half prepared for:
no chance for you to fit in,
to grace a movement, your only alternative
was greatness.

How human that was. Though I myself
am still engaged in various schools and causes,
only too innocent as I perceive them,
yet I will concede, the mind is most poetic
not in intimacy, but in reaching out:
poetry is the invasion of darkness,
not settlement, not familiarity.
Now that I shall not see you at the weekend
conference with your new translators,
surprised, even hurt, to have been disinvited,
I am also relieved: because we share no future,
at last I am free to tell you, face
to absent face, how much your gift,
of loneliness inhabited, has meant.

LETTER TO PAUL ALPERS

December 1985

Dear Paul,
    The other night, our Wednesday
dinner at the Hayes Street Bar and Grill,
you talked of pastoral, *a space
for exchanging song*, as in
Virgil's Ninth, *the discussion
of social upheavals on the road.*   Alpers '89 4
I count it as a gift
that we have done that, both in our
annual walks about the flanks
of Mount Tamalpais (how to forget
you lost at sunset on the dark north slope,
our calling *Paul*, the woods and shrubs resounding,
Svetlana's prospects of a fatal frost,
our brief, pastoral anxiety?), but more
to have exchanged translations of the Eclogues,
a project solidly accomplished, in your case;
in mine, another unfinished
folie de grandeur.
                    And nonetheless
a communication, the more certain
because we came from different places,
saw pastoral differently (for you
a sometime Harvard Fellow and a Jew,
the continuity of shared particulars,
conventions, done violence to, for me
with my solipsistic Canadian overview
from the artificial limits of the map,
the restorative, the *peace transcending words*,
what the Frankfurt School called radical nostalgia.)
Thus we too could feel this was a conversation
unprecedented as well as old, in space

never quite so defined. To be sure, we share much else:
both writers, teachers, close witnesses
of the Sixties' tear-gas, roles preferred
because so little is implied; imagine
if you were a doctor now, or I
a diplomat.
      At least you know
you are a teacher, for me,
even in my fifties, it is still
a postponement of decision. And perhaps
now that *faute de mieux* I accept
it as my only calling, I teach worse.
Once, as a mere job, I summarized
the classics, and defined
as easily as A) B) C)
what in Dante to remember. Now
I explore each author like a cave,
not so much interested in the poet's design
as in the opposite, to show how deep
the darkness at the end of each *couloir*,
the unpleasant proximity of death
more and more audible upon my lips
in my increasing gestures towards silence.
Part of myself objects that these are secrets
not to be discussed *devant les jeunes*,
whose chief concern is notes to be remembered,
not incoherent ramblings.
Part of me yearns to strip away
all shared hypocrisy, in the name of candor
revealing darkness.
      But death also reveals. That night
before *Der Rosenkavalier*, as we shared
Malpèque oysters and a chardonnay,
not unmindful of the nearby homeless,
St. Anthony's kitchen, the vents for sleeping warm,
yet reasonably at ease with luxury,
you told me of that extraordinary moment,
for you an escape from the last World War,

for me a change in it, when Primo Levi
from memory recited from Ulysses'
rebellious speech, *Considerate*
la vostra semenza — Think of your breed:
You were not made to live like brutes,
But to follow virtue and consciousness,
to a week-long acquaintance,
a fellow-prisoner at Auschwitz.
                                        Not,
as Irving Howe had misremembered, *when put to work*
scraping the inside of a petrol tank
but later, outside, the sun
drawing *a smell of paint from the greasy earth*
and in the distance, the *Carpathians*
covered in snow. A pleasant walk. We spoke
of our houses, of Strasbourg and Turin,
of the books we had read, of what we had studied,
of our mothers. And then
the canto of Ulysses. Who knows how or why?
As if I also was hearing it
for the first time: like the blast
of a trumpet, like the voice of God.
For a moment I forget
who I am and where I am.
And then the soup line: cabbages and turnips
Kaposzta es repak.   Levi 117, 121

        You praise in this
the pastoral conventions of *a space*
for exchanging song, just as in
Virgil's Ninth, *the discussion*
of social upheavals on the road.   Alpers '89 4
I think of epic, a turning-point
more historical than my reconstruction
of Mengele's and Barbie's escapes
to their post-SS careers. This is a truth
from and for history, that when the dead
press in upon us, a trumpet sounds,
not to all, certainly, but those

favored with an ear to hear it,
like the *wild blasts of music* Wordsworth heard
in the midst of terrible events
in Paris, the tribunals of the just:
a different perspective on despair,
more urban, not lightened for an hour
by a landscape *under a clear June sky*.

      You and I were spared,
guiltily, that ear's arousal.
But now, your parents dead,
my father, no more children home,
the absence quietly fills with temporal music,
not apocalyptic, the black lake ice
crackling on Quebec December nights,
but gentler, losing that angry pain
that comes from expectation, more calm,
like the white morning frost that tinkles
as it melts in the California sunlight.

      Or for ourselves, these dinner conversations
on opera evenings, more deeply felt,
less social, now that our wives,
more fully settled in their own careers,
are mostly absent, their season tickets sold
to strangers at a loss. If the risk of age
is that shared knowledge can become a fortress
inaccessible to the young, the greater need
for us in comfort to talk things through:
not mere grievance now, but things that last.

      Ulysses' speech, for instance: you saw
as Irving Howe did not, the irony
that these rebellious lines should so outlast
Dante's attempt at pious condemnation,
become a message, not of Christian drowning,
but of survival, though Levi saw
two breeds himself in the huge Auschwitz
experiment: the shipwrecked and the saved.
Dante for me is altered now, no choice,
teaching it again, but to advance

what Blake admired in Milton, the rebel voice
in epic I once feared, emancipation
at odds with order, those mad designs
for sobering empire, just as Whitehead first   Whitehead 228
and then Marcuse, made Dante's *gran rifiuto*   Marcuse 149, 170
into a virtue. (In time of course we lose
that need to fear our own emancipation.)
     Was it not from you I learnt
that no literature could be trusted
except that mistrusting itself?
The task in Rich's *Sources:*
womanly, powerful, yes, because self-searching,
but also (for this reason?) self-defensive,
as when she talks of commonplace
self-recognitions we should expect,
her father's *suffering of the Jew*
as if seen by an expert, with *a lens*
womanly, powerful. Her conscious theme
the thread between a "destiny" and a mission,
her split roots of Jewishness and freedom
with talk of books, ideal societies,
alien in the woods that I grew up in
where Hebrew names — like Bethel, or Mount Pisgah,
displaced the silenced Indians, at the whim
of Miltonic Zionists. Her poem half-intends
her Jewish separateness, *something more*
than food and humor, outside the dated
Yankee fantasy of *settlement*, belied
by the caved-in sugar-house, its boards
like *pewter in the dew*, the industrious
stone fences through returning forest, the dour
hold-outs against inexorable displacement
by defeated French-Canadians.
                But the poem confirms,
surely, a sense of being, all of us,
alien invaders, in our search for freedom
dispensing tyranny, the French in time
to mitigate the Iroquois intrusions.

Was it so ironic that Bethel bred
the Book of Mormon, or that Pisgah's view
was once again *a promised land,* for holiness,
whose inheritance was, shall we put it, questionable?
With such a birthright, should we not mistrust
any *mission*, even hers (and ours) to find
an end to suffering?
      Dilemma: how admit
through literature the search for emancipation
and not, at the same time, privilege its authors
with a *power* which, the moment it leaves self
and becomes restrictive, rises up against us?
What "great" authors do can be compared
to the impact of "great" nations; nonetheless
they share the power to escape from "greatness."
This is my struggle now with Ezra Pound,
not your favorite author, whose crimes
were all of them self-betrayals, whose defense
was like his crimes a sickening self-torment
offering, from its inner darkness, refutation
in verse to his false rhetoric. Yet perhaps
not deep enough, could not be deep enough,
but the moment we say that, we admit
what others claim, that literature
is no less answerable than any language,
the question being, when we deconstruct,
whether we are adding, or subtracting,
meaning to amplify, or to destroy
the writing which emerges out of struggle
and is, and is not, part of it.
Forgive me.
      You yourself, in your fine book
on *pastoral questioning of pastoral*, hence Alpers '79 236
on nothing less than literature itself, discern
a doubleness in Virgil, *the impartial
interplay of opposites, the web*
beneath the public stoic surface, of *antithetic
symbols, of tensions and oppositions*

never finally resolved. The man, Alpers '79 247-8
in short, whom Matthew Arnold,
in his sensitive self-hatred, called *not adequate*
for the *thorough mastery* of his Roman world. Alpers '79 246
You show how this was learned
in the rehearsals of the *Eclogues*, but I teach
how all epics of the canon, including Homer,
reveal this doubleness, this deeper
counter-current of cross-intention, how perhaps,
all literature, not just pastoral, reveals it,
but epic, because it has a broader surface,
the impurity, the laborious distortion
of straining to harmonize the social order
has a shadow current more rebellious.
Mistrust intention, but accept the poem,
precisely the residue. What means, and is.

This once was hopeful, each latest epic
freeing us from the dogmas of the last,
like Pound, annihilating Milton's *sin*;
gnarled faiths, the legacies of divided pasts,
dissolved and merged in poetry, and hope.
But how much good is liberated hope
in this century, when the warring creeds
are all of them creeds of emancipation,
and the biggest, liberation from the past?
And for us, if dissolution becomes a threat
to the liberating search I once believed in
for a good society, will we not be left
in a vast academic bureaucracy,
industrious, self-depriving, oblivious
to love? Mistrust intention,
but not the dream, to follow consciousness
by venturing higher, out of our worm-like state.

You yourself, as we drove over the bridge
up into the sunset, joined the attack
on a unifying canon, those few books
Harvard had dignified. In a sense
you seemed to attack yourself, the English major

you helped design, with its classical requirement
(that fatal onus for my class on Homer),
the same Harvard you find out-of-date
and to which you send your children. Without a canon
how can we explain our privilege
of teaching what tradition pleases, not
what demanding crowds or central planners choose?
The one privilege I would defend,
not because of what we know, or even
what poets mean to know, but from belief
faithful without a faith, in the deep
patterns, still emerging, not intended,
the writing that the waves leave on the sand
that will be heard again, in the next
war to end all wars, a blast
of inexplicable music.

NOTES

Alpers, Paul J. "Pastoral and the Moments of Reprieve." *Threepenny Review* (Summer 1989), 18-19.

Alpers, Paul J. *The Singer of the Eclogues*. Berkeley and Los Angeles: University of California Press, 1979.

Levi, Primo. *Survival in Auschwitz: the Nazi assault on humanity*. Translated from the Italian by Stuart Woolf. New York: Collier Books, 1961.

Marcuse, Herbert. *Eros and Civilization*. Boston: Beacon Press, 1955.

Rich, Adrienne. *Sources*. Woodside, CA: Hayeck Press, 1983.

Whitehead, Alfred North. *Science and the Modern World*. New York, Macmillan, 1925.

LAURENTIAN ECLOGUES

THE LOON'S EGG

On the eighth day, the rain stopped before dusk
Letting in sun. We canoed again at last.
The trip ruined, we could stop where we liked,
And picked, from the shadow of a tiny island
Like a ship going under, this loon's egg.
Its oval rested in our aching hand,
Turned amid chaos with a strange precision:
An orb, turned inside out, like an astrolabe
Of dimly remembered mists and galaxies
Sepiaed on dull blue. Dull, white within,
It had been broken into. Perhaps a snake
Lubric as night, had wound within its toils
These mottled stars, then with its wily bite
Had let in the catastrophic light,
As if this loon not to be hatched were Time,
And we Time's infants, the grey dust within
This ghostless orrery within our hand.

No trail came near. The jagged waterline
Unchanged in that water since the glaciers,
Rain, snow, wind safely cherishing what we
Could crush in an instant by mistake. O yes
Talk was strange there, letting in contagion;
Yet we listened to it as if we were miles away
Or years. Nor can I tell you, using words
Furbished from savage industry and war,
Why this inky egg-tint we have no legend for
Rests in my memory as if innate,
Vast, and secular. Is this the universe,
A shell, love's broken O, a voided beauty
The lover dare not look inside? The stones
Were almost worn away; the three short pines

Looked stunted in its formal presence; while the
Berries in the moss and outcrop were
Blue and sweet, as any in Ouareau Township.

    If you cross over from the narrow high
    end of Lake Antostigan (itself
    two days in) where there is some
    maple that was never cut, and wade down
    six miles of creek which is mostly mud and alders
    so dense even the aerial maps have missed them,
    and then, below the cliffs, more like a
    staircase the canoe is handed down
    since the high portages were never cut
    and the rest blown over in the hurricane
    before the war (you could, I suppose,
    come up the other way, with ropes
    around the falls, if you were mad enough)

You will stand above our fireplace and, like us
Seven years ago, perhaps will break off speech,
Kneel, and look down upon
This broken relic of a mottled world
We cannot really know, how hard we try,
Yet carry in the hollow of our heart:
The loon's egg

ARGENTEUIL COUNTY

'Shall horses run upon the rock? Will one plow there with oxen?'

—Amos vi. 12

Freely the dead bracken breaks to your stride
Now that at last the birds and leaves have gone,
Smells of wet granite stay in the mildewed wood,
The tabernacle of the sumac's torch,
Extinct, throws its frail shadow on the groundfrost.
Through the thick bush I trace a fieldstone wall
And line of cedar rails, now rich with lichen,
To a log cabin, smelling of animal,
Scored with the weathered names of the sleeping hunters,
A farmhouse once: the dying apple-tree's
Three shrivelled winesaps, cankered and gone wild
But sweet, delay me through the years;
The drop-jawed mailbox with its Biblical name,
Inspired by the wind, discourses like a skull.

The stones these settlers thought to use for fences
Lay in these valleys heavier than their wishes.

And this is Shrewsbury: two dirt roads meet,
A whitewashed church shines in its little parish
Of fenced-in lawn.
I think, *It's Sunday*, and I seem to see
A horse, a buckboard, and a clergyman
Come out of the east —
              He speaks. *God sent you, boy.*
Here, hitch my horse, you'll find some oats in the sack.
City-helpless, holding in my hands
These nervous reins, I feel how strange we all

Become in this land of improbable encounter
Not even the horse belongs to.

He opens his doors out, and will somewhat loudly
Harangue the township: *Brethren, by His love*
A vine was planted in the wilderness
Of human strivings, and the boughs thereof
Were comely, and the voice of praise was heard.
But now, O parents, look to your tender fruit.
The fox is among you, and your sons go down
Into the smoke of Mammon and are lonely.
While we let Papists (here his tired lips purse)
Buy out this land which was our fathers' birthright.
Let us pray. It's cold. His anger breaks off oddly
Spent on one father and his sixty-five-year-old son
Who've driven up from Lachute in their Chevrolet
To keep ceremony.

A rain begins in the marsh. They drive me to town
Through the tall choirs of maples, which have witnessed
This old settler tote out when a boy
One hundredweight of potash fifty miles.
His uncle was Bear Morrison, acclaimed
In someone's *Tales of Argenteuil County*,
Who with his gun-butt fought and killed a bear.
To farm here took hard liquor. Now they say
That through the streets of Shrewsbury they've seen
Stretching from the church to beyond the hill
Three hundred buckboards at an Orange gala
The whole night through.

We progress. The son keeps talking. *Now the Province*
Has brought in electricity, keeps the roads open
In winter, more roads than we broke ourselves
In the old days, though there's not six farms left

From here to Morin Heights. My only boy
Sharecrops in California. There's more to be had
On relief there, than ploughing with a team
In this boulderdrift. Nevertheless I tell you
A man was happy scything his own field
Or raising barns for neighbours. Dances, wakes,
We fixed for ourselves, took turns at the reeveship,
And lived by customs we could call our own.
Now we just come up to the farm on Sundays
To see all's well, and maybe in the spring
Cut us a little lilac.

On the way to town
We passed a dozen cars bringing out deer.
In the gloomy resonance of rain and shooting
I thought of his forebears and their vanished music
And stared at the windshield-wiper's weary sweep
Against the dusky rainlight turning to snow
As our lamps traversed a desolate beaver meadow,
Labrador tea, dead elms, and two scared eyes.

RUMORS OF NO LAW

I HATE MODERN POETRY

a hot season
the moon glowing at dawn
in the crimson west

thank god there are
some secrets not easily arrived at

the flower children
across the bay
looking for god

Susan Atkins
the Manson slave
has described it

I was dance
he came up behind me
put his hands on my hips

for the rest of us brains
in the same period
there was Carlos Marighella

the I Ching
Michel Foucault
yin and yang spinach

a chance for new words

all I could think of
to tell them

twenty thousand of them
in the Greek Theater
for Cambodia

was facts

DYING IN

dying on the grass
in front of the chancellor's building
for Charlie Schwartz's anti-weapons protest

brings back confused
memories of the wartime sixties
hitting the dirt before we realized

these were just wooden bullets
and then walking back through tear gas
to teach a class

lying here
and watching the neutral passers-by
scale the vertical asphalt

I feel neither
the old embarrassment at being
at right angles to most people

with brief-cases
nor, and this is the spooky part
that steam of comprehending anger

only the warm
smell of the grass beside my nose
saying, *come back here every now and then*

ALMOND TREE

for weeks you lay
dismembered in our garden

your trunk
glowed in the January dusk
a wet plate of sap

now I am in this pit
wrestling with your amputated roots
I embrace you you will not budge

on the south side your flesh
the color of disturbed almond
makes my axe ring and ring

on the north my spade cuts through punk

there was no room
for your dark blighted foliage
almond tree

         though I admit
also to being fortyish
by no means as green as I was

just because I too
am weighed down with mortification
which does not start from the roots but
is absorbed through leafwork

the more determined I am
to extirpate you
you made frail by smogs are to be my victim

through sweat and rain
I see my children
jump for the clean chips

just because in my office
where for years I have studied
there is no evil that my bright
rarely-used axe can hack at

here I swing it deep in the sloppy mud
and my splattered body athwart the pit
feels at last the tug of your buried taproot

I embrace you blindly and
with a small throatlike noise
you bring us both over

MY SON ROWING

The heavy oars stagger towards me
drop with a splash
he sits down

wrestles them slowly back
until open-mouthed he stares
straight up at the sky

again he must stand to push
the dripping blades back where he cannot see them
and squirm to keep his two wrists together

my job is to say *slowly*
a controlled stroke is what matters
speed comes from thrust not rate

his face, in school
so slow to register instructions
is fierce with study

and now his oars go deep
as if thankful for the water's firmness
to be found and striven against

he stretches full-length, propped
only by two small
whirlpools

echoing the noise made once
by ancestors fishermen
who had surely a song to space

the grunt and wheeze of these oarlocks
the measure for a man's arms being
no more then than today

and as once or twice
his small arms find that exigent measure
he breaks to an untoothed smile

we jerk forward
gaining less on the austere
banks of the city around us

than on his childhood and my prime
slipping in matched pairs of puddles
neatly down our wake *Good*

I say His small brother
mindless of stench and light rain
hears with admiration

the boat in the wind
sing and begin to move

TALKS AT THE YENAN FORUM

Question — and you thought yourself a revolutionary
    your sensibility caught
    the frail smoke of bombs in a woman's eyes

    the reflection of a river
    not the current

    Love is a concept
    Fundamentally we do not start from a concept
    but from objective practice

    the students in France
    have shown the workers how to change life
    Social practice and its effects are the criteria

    said *You have to maim a horse*
    on stage to remind these people

    the peasant
    knows how to endure
                    a slow fury
    is released in the blasts of saboteurs

    Genuine love of mankind
    will be born only
    when class distinctions have been eliminated

    now they have cut down the trees of the Rue Gay-Lussac
    for barricades

    why is it still green in your soul?

Response — I knew a woman with so big a heart
        you could walk through it like a ravine

    there is not a phrase
    that has not been polluted
    we must climb upstream

    to the source of revolution
    the waters gathering in granite pools
    high above the city

    yes we shall need all our wits
    to become unintentional

    where the silence of two mouths
    breathing together

    issues in naked words

SORA

ever since Sam
put chickens out in the reeds
and willows behind her trailer

in the draw below the hot spring
the birds have not been the same
the snipe comes tap tap

pecking beyond where
we sunbathe while the comic
sora whom according to Robbins

one never sees
somehow thinks it's a chicken
works the grass by the pool

if we could only believe
that likewise some natural
atavistic grace could revive

in the brains of Sam's chickens
how we would look forward
to that probable day

our own naked children
will grow by some pool like this

yes! even though this morning
just before the lucid
colorless desert dawn

the shadow of the eastern mountains
beginning to drop
on the western wall of the Inyos

we flushed a sharp-shinned hawk
which dropped from its talons
into a willow-branch

the dappled plumage
red meat skew-headed neck
and reproachful eye

of the too-trusting snipe

PREPOSITIONS OF JET TRAVEL

For Malcolm Caldwell, d. December 23, 1978

i
In a dawn so clear
        the only clouds visible
        are on the far sunny side

of the Sierra
        as we glide down
        I strain to detect

not just our shadow
        but the shadow
        of the condor

between the snowy summits
        of the Los Padres forest
        and through all the valleys

of Los Angeles
the green and the burnt canyons

ii
the pilot says
        we are to pick up the jet stream
        above Interstate Ten

in one corner
        of the beige wilderness
        of San Jacinto

is pasted the green stamp
      of Palm Springs

down there the butlers
      of Walter Annenberg
    and the U.S. Secret Service

are doing their futile best
      to prepare for the arrival
of the Shah

    iii
everything
     has somewhere to get to

at 1000 feet per second
      with this shred
   of maraschino on my fork

we drift across
      the sluggish
   Rio Grande

    iv
merely thinking about it
      is not going to change
   the crook of that lake

but if I could get
      the pilot drunk enough
   (I must be getting drunk myself)

who knows and if
        there is a clear enough sunset
     who knows if we could not drift a little south

catch a glimpse of Cuba
        before setting down
     in the lights of San Juan

     v
this does not put us on a level with
        the conscious
     takers of risk

like Malcolm
        whom they found and shot
     in his bedroom in Phnom Penh

yet looking down
        at the snowlines on desert peaks
     making a tapestry of horizons

we must make it meaningful
        after the crash in San Diego
     there was a hole

the shape of a dutifully
        bent-over man
     in the house's opposite wall

and absurd near-silence
        as when Fay's sister drowned
     the exhausted survivor

the gently bobbing canoe

vi

in the monocled
      notes and comment
    of the *New Yorker*

I read that the coup de grace
      of the non-violent
    Iranian demonstrators

was to imitate
      one of the wildest
    Berkeleyan fantasies

to physically embrace
      the soldiers in the streets
    and put carnations

in the barrels of their guns

even though this story
      does not seem fated
    to have a cheerful ending

it is good
      they have reminded us
    that to be historic

we have to keep in mind
      what we were and what we wanted
    in the first place

vii
this symposium
          in New York
          will be thousands of more words

about the assassination
          of John F. Kennedy
          one has to admire

the silence
          of those who planted
          the two matching bullets

the poetry
of paranoia

and yet there is no excuse
          for the illusion
          that on planet earth

the rarely-violent
are no more than passengers

think of that nervous
          Air Force lieutenant
          in the rear of the auditorium

stumbling over his well-phrased question

we are not as futile as we might wish
          one has to explain
          at the private lunch

of the concerned Asian scholars
   the presence of the
  self-invited

tenth guest

  viii
and now
   the dangled stars
  good night Malcolm

the world must not forget
   you were also a humorist
  having had a childhood

we all have
   sooner or later
  to deplane

as Maimonides said
   prophecy
  is open to anyone

living is more than life
go to sleep now

four inches
   from my left eye
  it is fifty below

ALAMERE

For Maylie, Cassie, John

It has to be merely symbolic
descending in the fog
along the former course of the nearby
waterfall through the
dry cleft in the rockface

to the wind-drifted beach
empty except for
three stiff parkaed
faces waiting for sleep

by a bleached fir trunk
we make a sand hearth
from friable cliff shale and
with cupped hands cherish a small
orange flame in the nest of thorns

its small wind-threatened dance
in the recalcitrant flotsam
nothing beside those bonfires
our ancients exulted to

or even those in the north
which before marriage in prophetic
clouds of steam I would defy
Quebec rainstorms with

and yet it stirs
from those sibilant fibers
a soft rage of electrons

like irrevocable music
which might have escaped from us
if we had not gone on through life

and it is comfortingly
adequate to the small T-bone steak
cradled in our potlid

we shall eat with cold red wine
before the long night
of luminous amniotic breakers

EAGLE

The moral of the story
        is to have become aware
    of the eagle

not the flat tree-eagle
        of Joachim of Flora
    with a beak-root and tail feathers of lilies

flying over our weather
        like the end of a cloud across the sun
    to dazzle at the last grand moment

nor the golden eagle
        flying low to challenge us
    from his usual eyrie

when we roped over the snow
        near the top of Mount Thompson
    no! this eagle

is for ourselves to take pride in
        it is this large space brilliant
    as magnesium in the clouds

we have fashioned like a 747
        to enter and leave
    what we called the present

we may ignore the small voice of a pilot
        or someone announcing the weather
    at O'Hare Field the point of having

drunk our champagne above the Sierra
        while advancing into
      the darkening thunderheads of night

houses and cities lost sight of
        was to be free to come or go
      the head keenly aware of the nearby hand

MOUNT TAM

MOUNT TAM

i

MISCHIEVOUSNESS

Bushwhacking up under the greasewood,
we followed the deer tracks and the water-hose
up from Green Gulch to the ridge
where we could see Mount Tam in one direction,
the comic Transam pyramid to the south
between the rounded treeless hills, and in the bay
the immobile fleets of slanted sailboats,
and all this time

the gentle January breezes every which way
off the broad pear-colored Pacific
with its clouds held back, allowing us
to eat unhurriedly our pilchards
and Monterey jack through our discussion
of locking into the waltz's form
and *the mischievousness beyond form,*
the dying man breathing
against Baker Roshi's count, the Zen
tennis player still wanting to win,
the frisky dogfights over Hanoi
(even a Bodhisattva can be mischievous),
with our January parkas open
our hair teasing innocently our eyes,
yes all this time

the tick under my armpit
was nibbling its slow clockwise toil

into its pleasure, slowly intruding its head
under my tight-packed skin, as we marched
downwards to where the broad ridge ended
under the bisection of sea and great sky,
feeling at one, outside ourselves
with our well-being, the easy downhill hike,
and Baker Roshi's lecture, the way we saw
our 500-foot-long shadows, across from us,
silhouetted on the steep opposite hill,
to make us as small as, yes, two fleas
on this sleeping hip and flank,
it was working

its way into me, it too was immersing
itself in the richness of being, growing so fat
and at home that next morning, when
my whole side ached, as if I had been chopping wood,
I looked, and mistook it
as part of myself, an inflamed mole
infected now, a ring of deep red
like yesterday's sunset, not recognizing
the contest of wills and antibodies, which would win
by converting the other into meat,
with the insistence of the hepatitis
four years ago which has rearranged my life:
O Zen tick

who carried me off from Green Gulch, even after
Maylie twisted you carefully anticlockwise
out with a pair of tweezers, the great
corona of inflammation remained,
pinpointing our non-existence,
our shared Sunday in Marin,
of which company you by a little
were the first to go.

ii

TIDE

When I said *The therapist*
thinks you must have a resistance
to therapy there was a long
silence but later when we
angled across the parking lot
you said my wanting to share
my therapy *warmed your heart*, however
at that very moment we caught sight of
the waves breaking in front of us
over our heads. The dotted line of pilings
in the sand, the grotesquely angled water meter
and open-mouthed garage high in the air
framed where the house had been till Wednesday;
I stood next door on the hastily rigged
planks out to the cement-block seawall
and felt under my feet the thud
of the white go-for-it-all-now surf.
    We never did get back to your confession
of being sloshy inside. We drove up past
the backdrop of remote skyscrapers,
icebergs among the dolphin clouds and hills,
and looked down on the sea's earth-fringe, it looked
so regular we could see nothing happening.
We were more aware of the four bluebirds,
the flock of goldfinches who flew,
suddenly, without any warning, into the oak.
    How secure, making lunch in the crag's cleft,
even though the bread, if not balanced right
might bounce down, down to where the kestrel hovered.
Although we agreed that it was *no more than flying,*
a sense of form which had nothing at all to do with

the form of the oak-tree we were flying into,
sitting above the brightly curved horizon,
with the moon tucked away beneath, its closest ever,
how swank and weird it was to be chewing sardines!

iii

AFTER THE BRAQUE SHOW

This Sunday you are in *sesshin*.
It is good. I am forced to inhabit
the hillslopes of my mind
the ones I usually walk through quickly
to get somewhere else, that has
more exotic flora, hopefully not yet seen,
but in fact one soon runs out
of the need for different experience,
the new airport, the new Holiday Inn.
    I have finished the morning paper. I can
go swim in the February ocean, revisit
the Braque show, study his *Studio One*
that shows his canvas of the familiar black pot
resting against an unfamiliar white one
flatter and more intense, like the great birds
that return from nowhere into his last frames.
He had reached the age he could afford
to look in on his own grand style, as a quotation:
once the constraint, now the letting go.
If I return there, it will be to leave,
to step into the rain, and see
beyond the columns of the courtyard
the dim guanoed seacliffs of Marin.
    But that was a week ago. Optimistic,
we went on to eat squid in a Thai restaurant.

Encouraged by the novel food, I warned
If we continue to work on our problems
expect more tears and pain, like this morning's
and you thought, incorrectly, I was leading up to
some new disastrous revelation. I only meant
that fear we always carry inside ourselves,
less dangerous, more unspeakable. But you broke off
our hike to Land's End, just as we'd almost arrived at
the point of the journey, the steps down to the beach.
And I believed you:
that rather than walk through a wet city
you preferred to go home and play Brahms.

   That evening, for the first time in months,
I hardly spoke at dinner. Luckily
Ricardo the Venezuelan and Shi-mei
from Inner Mongolia had just moved in
to the children's empty rooms. I wished
she would sing Chinese, but her song,
almost familiar, was *Pignals*.
Pignals? *Birds of peace*. Oh, pigeons —
and Ricardo guessed it: *La Paloma*. After all
that's how most of us keep going: at school
my new program in Peace Studies,
your new Strategic Therapy at the clinic.
It's almost as if by now it is
where we have just been we fear the most.
                          Today
I don't want to do something, not even to think.
Sitting here I can feel
my self resting against its shadow. Did I tell you
what Ann said about my dream
of driving too fast down the snowy hill
in the too large station-wagon,
and after telling Allan Gotlieb to slow down
(that part of me up front, too much a captain),

we saw in the ink-black brook beside us
big dormant fish in the just-thawed pools
like salmon in poaching-pans (or that bass last March
struggling upstream, as these were not,
in a creek so small it could not stay under water)?
She said *it reminds me of the ice you said*
she likes to hide her feelings under; and I
agreed: *in that case, it might mean*
her slowing us down last week was a good thing.
(After trying, then not trying:
like night vision, oblique to the small star,
a chance for the dark to become visible.)

   I like today's quiet. I might go back
to the familiar empty slopes west of Mount Tam
where we sat two weeks ago, for no other reason
than to wait, as we did not, for the timid deer
at evening-time, in sixes and twelves,
to come out and graze.

iv

FOG

[A]

We have parked just under
    the roof of cloud
  the trail goes in and out

past the the blue ceanothus
    and redwood porticoes
  the rare pink orchids

under the Douglas fir
    then saws like the fern's edge
  along the bare knuckles

of the western slopes
        before climbing into whiteness
    snatches of landscape here and there

sunlight not far below
        off the flooded parking lots
    of Stinson Beach

and above us nothing
        but two hooded figures
    hiking back out from the stream

larger than life above us
        as if strung from the sky
    on two invisible threads

like angels?

    [B]

lunch over the crest
        in the dripping forest
    brook silted and overflowing

just like in Canada
        the logs and hectic moss glowing
    Have we changed after twenty years?

I retort that your tastes are new
        mine not. You say, *I was younger*
    and I, *even before you I was the same*

scuds of mist drifting through
        the canyon dissolving in spring mist
    like the Chinese dragon in the water glass

beside my bed when I was six and sick
        the feverish colors of my crayon box
    the street beyond my bracken-frosted window

a comfort to hear the firs drip
        I prick my finger
    as on the crabapple thorn

I inserted into the folding arm
        of my parents' pre-war Victrola
    Now you are speaking again

of the need for growth
        Why would one want to escape
    the needle's retreating point

in the shrill groove of time?

        [c]

even going back down the trail
is a form of advance

the rusted upside-down Pontiac
        its burst springs at rest
    speaks to us from our recent past

I used to complain that we never talked
        whether from custom or desire
    the fact is

talk merely covers over
what the deep mist reveals

V

THE EEL

[A]

Intolerant of the unexpected,
you did not want to stop for the
dead drums and flags of the children's
Chinatown parade (*Why is it*

a Buddhist cares so much what she does on Sundays?
I asked), but when we saw the long queue
for the puppets at the Museum, you decided
not to join that boisterous family crowd:

it's good to see your face slowly give in.
That's how we got to buy the eel
for Shi-mei. The young man netted it
out of the tank, hammered

a spike through its tail into the block, and,
inserting a knife at the anus, pulled
steadily upwards to the neck, his finger
afterwards expelling the guts; I watched

that eye, commenting, even angry, then
the recognition, blankness, non-existence.

[B]

The ultimate genre
is thought to be tragedy;

but later, in the cafe,
how we startled

our Chinese-American waitress,
when our plastic

shopping-bag, still struggling,
flopped off its chair!

SPACE SONNETS

SPACE SONNETS

THE RAIN

As if lit by lightning in the storm
through the tall conference window, the high
single oak tree   crazily
blowing like a fountain in the rain

is here still; the global talk of peace
has passed on, as wars and peaces pass,
the flooded roads that kept us in that place
are dry again. It is the tree that rests

crazily   in this quieter place;
this quieter wind, that leaves undisturbed
the troubled windowpanes, finds in the ear

small leaves to rustle. All words come to this
the silence   and to discover
one more time, *There is this other world*

ii

Our terrors tell us nothing. Like cats
they become domesticated, but still are
strangers. As you said, *We cannot know
the contours of our feelings.*

And that other, deeper background, which should
by loss be visible, without enough
future to be afraid, how can we
be sure, or use our art to see it,

much less name, now that it is dark
and there are so many thoughts, there is
no more depth, the pepper branches fall

blackly like paper cut-outs out of night
against the western dim, where, this week,
remember,   brave men cried drowning?

iii

Though I slip away before dawn
in a Honda, and my headlights pick up
the Lycra buttocks of a jogger, nevertheless

what lies in my heart, the emotion
of stealth, must be akin
to Tristan's   or Giraut's

whose castle I could never find
as a young man in the Dordogne
in those innocent journeys through plum

blossom and Romanesque
Too well I now share with him
those white limbs in the dark

this sickle moon in the east
slicing the KPFA tower

iv

Because we were so certain that our love
was a transcendence   not a capture,
an entrapment   the words *want, acquire*,
even *enjoy*, all of them transitives

to larger selfishness, unfreedom,
till she, as we say, *objecting*, went away,
freeing us by her absence, to enjoy
this relaxation   It will come

as a surprise, the impulse like a breeze
to be a child, but a child no longer
impelled by want, *enjoying*   these

strange interstices between desires
          on the street, quite suddenly
walking nowhere   in particular,

V

(By escaping we bring back cleaner words)

Blocked again by the feral ghost of love
I go out and walk ankle-deep
in these wet subtropic petals out of trees
I do not know the name of

Within, though fantasies with strangers
still upset us with delights,
new kinship   those lonely ones
with whom we build again this tower of words

more fit for aging   and where desire was
the poetic lines   the flights
of fancy like an awkward pelican

soar a little   and must return
ferrying height back into the "self"
what, to escape from, we must become

vi

PLANH

So I have no more hair in back,
only a joke of a tonsure, that's o.k.
as long as I don't have to see it.

But this! to have nose-hairs in my ears,
a beard that is working up my nose,
to be *the arhat of the shaggy eyebrows*

Nature, butt off! if I ever thought
of you as parent, to be trusted,
forget about it. You should have quit

when you covered up my chicken-breast
with unasked-for curls. Now I want
the earmarks neither of a savage man

nor of a holy one   to be free
of all signs even that word *me*

vii

Two places familiar: the old one
where the woman walked, the flesh amazed
at its own danger, even this late time
a preface   to confusion

as we recall it in the rain
that keeps the bees in hive, too late
for the white drifting of almond petals
mindlessly blown back to the black ground;

this other, when she leaves, desire

which in that first place seemed being's fullness,
now   our failure to be breathing here

viii

And how describe the woods behind the words
when the controlling word is   *(silence)*
and all the rest at best transparencies
like dirty windows in the crowded wards

of language?   *sometimes in italics*
we cry out Tree! and there is both the tree
and someone speaking.   But poetry
where, not quoting, in quotation marks

we say "ourselves"   and the "self"
nothing else   but what we say
opens   the structure of disbelief

the task of the poet   nothing else
than clean this window that has no view
and when we look at it   no glass

ix

And down the huge swollen river blunder trees,
bits of houses, crates, patios, logs
with bobbing pelicans, a cat, a dog,
I envy them that rocking. It arouses

a memory   of peace,
forces passing through us, no voice
in this movement somewhere else,
the mouth not yet entrusted with the choice

to suck   or be free
then speaking   in first awkwardness
after cataclysm, intimacy

not repeatable. The animals, all of them
are looking downstream, as if they expected
that rest we have forgotten   the ocean.

MIDDLE KINGDOM

FROM LI BAI (LI PO)

BALLAD OF A YOUTH

A western youth come east to the Gold Market!
His silver saddled horse beats the spring wind.
The fallen flowers all trampled, where will he rest?
Smiling, he enters the Tartar concubine's wine shop

SITTING ALONE AT QINGTING MOUNTAIN

The high birds have all flown away
A lonely cloud drifts idly by itself
There is only Qingting mountain
We look at each other without getting tired

AUTUMN THOUGHTS

In Yanzhi the yellow leaves are falling
Alone, I look out on Paideng Terrace
No more jade clouds above the sea
Cicada sounds have come with the autumn colors

The Hun armies have gathered in the desert
The Han messenger has returned from Jade Pass
For you soldiers there will be no return
Vainly I lament the fallen orchids

ON HEARING THE SHU MONK CHUN PLAY THE LUTE

The Shu monk carries his Luyi lute
Down from Mount Emei's western peak.
He moves me with a sweep of his hand,
It is like hearing a thousand valley pines

My wayward heart is washed in flowing water,
The lingering tone becomes a frosty bell.
I do not see the Jade Mountain sunset,
How heavy are the darkening autumn clouds

WRITTEN AT JINLING PHOENIX TERRACE

On Phoenix Terrace phoenixes once roamed
Phoenixes gone, terrace empty, the river flows by itself
In Wu Palace grass buries the dark walks
Zhou dynasty talents have become old mounds

Three mountains half fallen beyond the blue sky
Two rivers split in two by White Egret Island
Floating clouds often can hide the sun
Chang'an not seen is what has caused my grief

THE FAVORITE BEAUTY OF KING WU, HALF DRUNK

The breeze wafts lotus fragrance through the palace
On Gusu Terrace the King of Wu is resting
Xi Shi, drunk, dances beautifully without strength
At the window, laughing, she leans towards the white jade couch

TWO POEMS BY WANG WEI

CROSSING THE YELLOW RIVER

A boat sailing on the great river,
the waters enormous, the horizon small.
Sky and waves suddenly split apart:
a district capital, ten thousand homes.

Closer up I see a city market,
perhaps even mulberry and hemp.
I look back to my native village:
The broad flood is joined to clouds and mist.

DEER PARK

In these empty mountains, I see no one;
only hear human voices echo.
Reflected shadows enter the deep forest,
again illumining the green moss.

FROM DU FU

MOONLIT NIGHT

(From His Captivity in Chang'an)

Tonight a moon in Fuzhou.
In her women's quarters, she looks out alone.
From afar I pity my sons and daughters
Who have no memory of Chang'an.

In fragrant mist, her cloud-like hair is moist.
In the clear beams, her jade-white arms are cold.
When shall we lean on the empty window-frame,
Moonlit together, traces of weeping dry?

FROM THE QINZHOU MISCELLANY

Myriad disordered layered mountains.
Lonely city in the mountain valley.
No wind: clouds rise from the frontier pass.
No night: the moon sets toward the frontier gate.

Why is our envoy late in his return,
Not yet back from the vassal lord's beheading?
Smoke, dust: I watch for hours alone,
The spent breeze ravaging my face.

Parted by death, there's an end to tears;
Parted by life: endless commiseration!
South of the Yangzi, there is a plague;
Of you, my exiled friend, there is no news.

So old comrade, you enter my dream,
Knowing we keep each other in our thoughts.
I am frightened — Is your spirit not alive?
And so long a journey — it cannot be fathomed.

Your spirit comes: the maple groves are green;
Your soul goes back: the frontier passes darken.
Now somewhere you are trapped in nets;
How is it you are here with wings?

The moonlight, setting, slants across the beam,
Reflections doubtful, the gloom uncertain.
The waters are deep, and the surf breaking high:
Don't let the sea-snakes drag you in!

IN GUIZHOU, REMEMBERING THE PEAR GARDEN COURT
DANCES AT A PERFORMANCE BY LADY LI

The Pear Garden dancers have dispersed like mist.
Her residual grace flares in the fading sun.
South of Golden-Grain Tomb trees are now arches.
On the wall of Qutang Gorge grass moans in the wind.

FROM SU DONGPO (1036-1101)

IMMORTAL NEAR THE RIVER

Drinking all night on the East Bank, sober then drunk again,
I return home: it must be three o'clock.
My house-boy's snoring is like the sound of thunder.
I knock on the door: no answer at all!
I lean on my staff, and listen to the river.

Long have I hated this body, not my own.
At what time will I forget life's cares?
Night is late, the breeze calm, the ripples smooth.
A little boat to drift downstream from here
On the river, and sea, the remainder of my life.

COAST TRAIL

COPPETT'S WOOD HOSPITAL

Closer to waking sleep
than I have ever been
on a clear day

I study the inside
of my breathing

and as I hear
myself snore

I am treated to the sight
of my body in pieces
like a modern sculpture

and in the intricate
white blurred ceiling
the insistent

faces of my grandmother in black
who smiles once again
at the beckonings of death

as absolute
as these nurse's hands
touching my pulse

what a bore
the doctor has just said
you have no reading glasses

I don't answer
but lie as still
as that long day in the Ventanas

when I listened to the changing
voices of rain
against our tube tent

and studied
with a dedication
not applicable to work

every leaf
of the black madrone above us
against the rainlight

DAWN IN MIAMI

(July 2, 1980)

Dawn in Miami
on the fifteenth floor of the Omni
I stand with bird glasses

and push aside the glass wall
just as the wind
has pushed aside the pre-dawn storm

The warm air
whips up my nightgown
along with waves

in the blue
postage-stamp swimming pool
below my right foot

There is nothing like a cloudburst
to clean the air
and empty the mind

for the first time I see
under the vistarama
of skyscraped thunderheads

beyond the ghetto
and even a bit
of unnecessary rainbow

the horizon
alerting me this
is the edge of life

Look! tinier even
in the portholes
of my wandering glasses

than the first opening car-door
above the wind-chased puddles
of the parking lot

or the small pond of traffic
where the blue diesels
of the Florida East Coast Railroad

shunt and strain
across U.S. One
to make up a train

Tinier than the first black
spume from the smokestack
of the snow-white Nordic Prince

or the law office
in the stunted nub
of the Alfred I. Dupont building

where I sweated yesterday
through a deposition
in someone else's lawsuit

Resorts International Inc.
vs. Straight Arrow Publishers
not worth a continental

flight from Oakland
absente justitia   justice being absent
tinier than all that

two nighthawks
dive and glide together
down across the boulevard

of broken palms

MAX SCHERR'S PARTY

November 5, 1981

I take off my black tie in the car
this is to be just a party
Max's last party
full of faces from the sixties
looking established — the college dropout
who thirteen years ago in the Heidelberg
was trying to explain to me about guns
the need to blow something up
now a success in Larkspur real estate
wants to be doing something about peace
as they are in Europe — a teach-in maybe?

> *with his barbed lance*
> *he tilted at what Sancho thought*
> *were just windmills*
> *but were sometimes fierce engines of war*
> *and sometimes balloons*

On the wall is the original pricelist
from Max's Steppenwolf
where for a buck or two you could sit
in the back and watch John Lion's
Magic Theater
with actors who've since made it on t.v.
Life was theater then
freedom to say and do anything
freedom even from words *Hrarrhhh!*
now John is a success
and had to leave early
but there's Dr. Hip in a dark suit

Fritjof has brought in a huge collage
of California filled with Barb photos
nude monitors at some sort of rally
Jimi Hendrix Kathleen Cleaver in her afro
a meditator with a picture of Gandhi
at the same People's Park fence
where a nightstick pins a demonstrator's neck
an advertisement Have You Seen This Child?
what looks like Mike Rossman's wedding
where you Raquel Max Scherr's daughter
were the only one not to strip like the rest
and at the bottom maybe smoke
from the Bank of America in Isla Vista
where George tells me he was busted
as soon as he showed the police his Barb credential

> *even now what is shared*
> *is not the external world*
> *but what we make of it*

Now kissed outrageously good-bye
by someone who then asks
Who are you?
I walk over to the silent cartons
of brittle flax-colored newsclips
and lift out a large photograph
of two stoned women looking askance
wearing only their Chaplinesque cravats
and bowler hats
I remember it
how it once turned me on
how in one sense the sixties
for all the nightsticks and tear gas
were a continuous party
the first time life was real

for those with the right black humor
You even died on Halloween
with the young trick-or-treaters
thronging to the door
out of the Reaganite darkness
Where do we go now Max?

> *into the future*
> *the surest thing after death*
> *where it has always been said*
> *there is a green country*
> *and libido will ride on reason's horseback*
> *as soon as we know our pleasure*

They broke the book in half
so that you might reread
the death scene of Don Quixote
you had enjoyed with your children
in the good days in Cuernavaca
before you became famous
but even so the book was too heavy for you
it is not your fault
that in the end it came down to
the tank of oxygen beside your bed
Raquel leaning close to your face
to say *Tell us what you want papa*
Squeeze my hand if you mean yes

"THE ACHIEVEMENTS OF F.R. SCOTT"

This is no dream — no more
than the dark descent was
into the cloud-stained inlet

peering through the small window
beyond my hand
balancing its small globe of wine —

to have arrived by taxi
and be ushered straight
into the huge ballroom

under enough lights
to extract confession
from the very furniture

past muscular guards
who turn back urgent-looking
men with letters and Hasselblads

past the dense crowd
of faces mostly familiar
except for their white hair

old notorious radicals
in dark three-piece suits
iconoclasts become icons

past the young careerists
who press into a circle
around the Prime Minister

I am led by the hand
to meet my mother
Marian who looks at me

meaningfully above the noise
as if to say
we shall talk soon

and then by some
determined stranger
into the presence of

my father Frank
to exchange greetings above
someone crouching with a microphone

longer than any instrument
a surgeon might use to probe
an old unhealing wound

but these movie cameras are friendly
searching for no more
than what is obvious

while the dark strait outside
is littered with the jetsam
of a country which still

just might be breaking up
and those few of us
guests from outside its borders

might add *not just the country
but law politics all
regulation of language*

tonight's program
of your life work in short
but that is the more reason

for us to celebrate
not just your achievements
but your generous failures

these too being marks
of wherever mind and life
have been energetic enough

to change each other
as in your case dear Frank —
and this is on the record —

even I tonight
to my surprise
forgive you

for having been my father
and the world of powers
you placed me in

it is like forgiving myself

REFLECTIONS ON A
FIFTY-EIGHTH BIRTHDAY

For David Gewanter

After forty years
time seems to accelerate
from shaving to shaving
but the face, despite occasional
white hairs around the edges
is virtually unchanged
and can still appreciate
the youth of what it sees.

Why then does my student friend
drag me excited
to the library display case
and expect me to be pleased
by the shots of poets
gripping the microphone

when the unthinking cameraman
from the grotesque height of our thighs
has caught the mellow truth
of Allen Ginsberg's wrinkles;
but put lines round my mouth,
depicted an unsure stoop,
taut cords in my neck,
and a glare behind my head
that looks like a bald spot
I know nothing about?

Still incredulous
I have to return, alone.
The ungenerous glass
intercedes with the faintest
ghost of my true reflection,
so white, all trace of age,
identity, gender, lost
for a moment only,
faint as the halo of breath
which from some childish need
to make a lasting impression

I smudge with my nose.

WAITING IN LINE

while you chatter you
reach out and take my hand
I am silent

even when you tickle
my palm slowly
and deliciously

I do nothing
but when you raise
my arm to your breast

something obliges me
to say *You know I don't know you*
you cover your face

your callow friend
in a tweed much like mine
says *girls from Fresno*

are real friendly
but nothing can quite undo
that moment of pleasure

we both got into
not even your
I'm sorry sir!

Here's hoping
someday perhaps
you will enjoy poetry

and be glad to read this

ZA-ZEN WINDOW

[RIGHT HAND: LIGHT]

i
The shadow of the bird
       hops along the wire
  shadow on the left wall

into the shadow of my head

ii
Are there still bees
       trapped in the wall, I wonder
  and next to my left knee

an answering buzz

iii
Again the first roof frost
       and new leaves break out again
  and turn yellow fall break out fall break out

breathing

iv
Hoitsu's new *Fu Hsin*
       calligraphy on the wall
   Is it *heart* or *mind*?

佛　　Buddha

心　　heart, mind

Without thinking, I smile

WINDOW ZA-ZEN

i

I light the candle
        its shadow in near silence
    circles below around

the blue linen dragons

ii

Treetops dull light
        the few inches
     between the candle inside

and the outside frost

iii

Having set the timer
        you turn off the light behind me
    from the inside of the glass

you again vanish

iv

left side
            wall of silence
    right side quiet

amphitheater of sound

BIRDNOTES

i

ROBINS

For Du Fu

Two robins charging each other
as I sweep by in my Honda

to the music of C.P.E. Bach
and then after the last turn

in the wooded canyon
the skyscrapers of San Francisco

their windows ablaze
from the dawn behind me I cannot see

ii

For Carolyn Merchant and Charles Sellers

It still flies where the ancient hogan's
roof has half collapsed (ten years ago
unchanged as was the chipping-ground)
now propped by someone's two-by-four

above the footprints down the volcanic mud
the desert wash that swirls past the glitter
of huddled RVs around the palms
of the upper hot spring, to the white flats

of the dry saline lake under the Inyos
the broken tramway of the mining company
the tall thin whirlwind of dust
from someone driving down out of Grapevine Canyon

UNTITLED

We must not exaggerate the effect
of my taking your clothes off
in the warm forest

on the far side of Mount Tamalpais
although undeniably it was freedom
to move barefoot on the soft pine needles

to make love for more than an hour
with you getting up in the middle
to "run around" which in practice

meant standing over me
in the chatter of the breeze
to admire the green ferns

the cool water of the brook
running through me from ear to toe
for as long as we wanted it

it is not that the thrushes'
songs were out of the caverns
of some different world

I remember only there were six
newts in the pool when I bathed
a deer's print in the mud next to mine

and at some point near the end
a large unknown butterfly
batting its emblemed wings

as it looked down at me
from the high summit
the clouds sailing on behind it

of my abandoned shoe

BAY TO BREAKERS

Yes I ran the Bay to Breakers
at the last minute, the pre-dawn unexpected
excitement drawing me out of my bed
at 6:00 a.m. I saw it as I wished
nowhere near the beginning or the end.
I too remember the shouts, the balloons,
the pretty fannies that passed me or I passed,
like the human six-packs, the foot, the burlapped trees,
or two Golden Gate bridges all passing each other,
the winos on carhoods croaking, *Go for it!*
the glorious downhill burst before the finish;
but more than any of these moments, I recall
the last unexpected gentle climb in the park
when the laughter and shouting ceased, and you could hear
instead of silence, the dead riverlike sound
of breathing, the dead quiet of life.
    That rests with me, just as after
the sprint at the close, the adjustment
to no more immediate goal to run for,
I soon came back to the finish-line, to watch
for almost an hour, the river of runners running,
and instead of the helpful cries, the loudspeakers,
the barkers, the four helicopters,
I heard what, with care, in today's normal traffic
I can still barely pick out, the almost dead
almost silence of life.

FOR DU FU

A simple love of the decent
Why this mean snarl under my breath?

From summers on lakes
where one never saw Indians

except to rent a canoe
I left to work for peace

and learned six languages
I have not used for years

Now I sit before dawn on this mat
and *dream the republic*

or in the alien sunlight
of this California back yard

in a shower of small privet blossom
a tree I first knew about from Virgil

despising this good life
which befell me by accident

I go on and on with the poems
that lose me my old good friends

When my eyes opened
to the vanities of my famous teachers

failed to get anywhere
in my love with the working class

and ceased to be jealous
when my wife left me for Buddha

how could I have foreseen
that in this last decade-long

pursuit of solitude
I would find you here, Du Fu?

ii

With our taste for allusion
we cannot understand each other

I will never have the eyes
to see your *Nan Shan*   South Mountain

even your willow and river
with its lone boat

are for you echoes of the Odes
and for me blue China

what then is *humanity*
if you must forever remain

mysterious inaccessible
like a wife?

LIZ AT SIXTY

Seeing you
in your enormous *bouffant*
no one has ever slept in
your face wide-eyed and masklike
as Mickey Mouse behind you
at *the portals of Disneyland*
opening *to the tune*
of "When You Wish Upon a Star"   San Francisco Chronicle 2/28/92

it is hard to remember
how each of us felt
you so fragile
with pure possibility
as you leant to your horse's neck
in *National Velvet*
the war almost over
your sex hidden in your jockey outfit

I watching with concern
from the back of the audience
throbbed with intensity
reserved for adolescence
at the deep bond created
by our dreams for the future

and would have written you
to explain how much we shared
had not that gross address HOLLYWOOD
separated us like a sword
where others would have read
my verses to you first
and not have understood

so we grew apart
I could see in that Albee play
as you bad-mouthed your drunk husband
Richard Burton (who by the way
I had met once when hitch-hiking
from outside Denham up to Oxford
you were right he wasn't good enough for you)
life had treated you cruelly
as he gave up Stratford
for the profits from B-movies
the high dreams dissolved
in higher-proof alcohol

now we have traded
that undeveloped future
for California's wealth
of malls and parking lots
I cannot retrieve those nights
I lay awake imagining
us walking together
innocently as two deer
through the lost autumn roadways
of the abandoned Laurentians
north of Montreal
now all fenced and gated
in vacation properties

we still need the word *dream*
if only for this
innocent hysteria
of a sixtieth birthday party
Dress for Fun, Jeans
Tres Casual your guests
saying *this is fabulous*   San Francisco Chronicle 2/28/92

and I see clearly
in the prodigious efforts of your face
to become timeless
as if in a mirror
this relentless exchange
of dreams for identity
life as *fabulous*
each of us imprisoned
in our Disneyland
of absurd efforts
to achieve remembrance

rather than confront
the ultimate question *What*
if there is nothing else?

YIN AND YANG

(At Dancing Coyote Beach)

For Ronna

    i

only deserts
     can sustain this intense
   celebratory

howling

    ii

behind
     the cracking embers
   the light plane's hum

the murmur of the stars

DOLL FETISH

"Her leaders now talked only of prodigies, monstrous deities
of every sort, and Anubis who barked like a dog"

— St. Augustine

Do you want it?
I asked
as with a healer's hands
you lifted the wing
of the broken barn owl
its breast soft
as ermine with black
tips to the barbed vanes
of each tiny feather
its round-eyed face averted
on that glass-strewn roadside
uselessly from its own destruction

and you astonished me
your sometime professor
by saying *No!*
my doll teacher says
you should never use
owl feathers in a fetish
they can mean death

A little later we saw
what we had come for
the paired sandhill cranes
jumping and bowing
in their courtship dance
under the low snow geese
the endless swans
creaking through the sky
as in the *National Geographic*

above the boats decoys
dockside Chevron stations
and dull shots like heartbeats
of the flooded delta
now crowded like a ghetto
for endangered species
the home once
of 30,000 Miwoks
according to the bait-shop brochure

But now reading St. Augustine
it is the owl I remember
beside the empty road
from whose death I learned
that the large china-faced doll
you would show me that afternoon

which took you months to make
after you dropped out of school
my class on Wordsworth
the program we'd both designed
for the university
to begin teaching peace

had not only human hair
joints a spinal column
brown eyes that followed you
around the room
as you rubbed noses
with your white parakeet Spike

but in some secret way
you learned in doll school
feathers bones
herbs eelgrass inside
for your slow healing
a fetish for each chakra
in order to ease

your rage from the grandfather
who when your mother came
to drive him to retirement
in sunny California

shot himself
with a rifle
in the garage

COAST TRAIL

For Fred and Betty Crews

You should know that a little way
ahead of you on the trail
there is a dead man

The wife and daughter
are waiting for the helicopter to come
or maybe horses

They are not in need
and the best thing
is not to disturb them

said the hiker
and we continued south
still watching for sea lions

naming the aromatic plants
to avoid both speech and silence
the more stilted our words became

the more one had a sense
they were being recorded
until it was a relief

to see the woman's white hat
just over the gentle grade
the kind of innocent sunhat

I wore when I was seven
in fields of asters like this one
she and her daughter were staring

up at the severe hillcrest
not at the sunlit blue sea behind them
with its frilly white waves

not at the slack body
in its store-new shirt and levis
the jaunty cloth cap covering

all but a strip of the
abalone-grey neck
our clumsy boots swerved

off the trail to avoid
as we pretended
we had somewhere else

to get to